Picture Perfect
Word Book

Language and Content Consultants
JoAnne Johnson • Kerri Morigaki • Joyce Elaine Smith

HAMPTON-BROWN

About the Consultants

JoAnne Johnson
Kindergarten Teacher
Woodbine Elementary School
Cicero School District
Cicero, Illinois

Kerri Morigaki
Bilingual Coordinator, Kindergarten Teacher
Park Western Place School
Los Angeles Unified School District
Los Angeles, California

Joyce Elaine Smith
ESL Teacher, Kindergarten–Grade 5
Mission West Elementary School
Fort Bend Independent School District
Sugar Land, Texas

Hampton-Brown
P.O. Box 223220
Carmel, California 93922
(800) 333–3510

Printed in the United States of America.

0-7362-0175-0
03 04 05 06 07 10 9 8 7 6

Contents

Themes

Animals

fin · · · ·

· · · · flipper

dolphin

raccoon

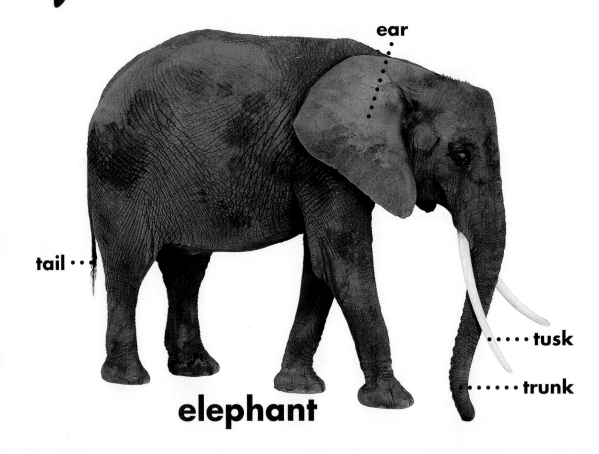

ear

tail · · ·

· · · · · tusk

· · · · · · trunk

elephant

wing

peacocks

paw

wolf

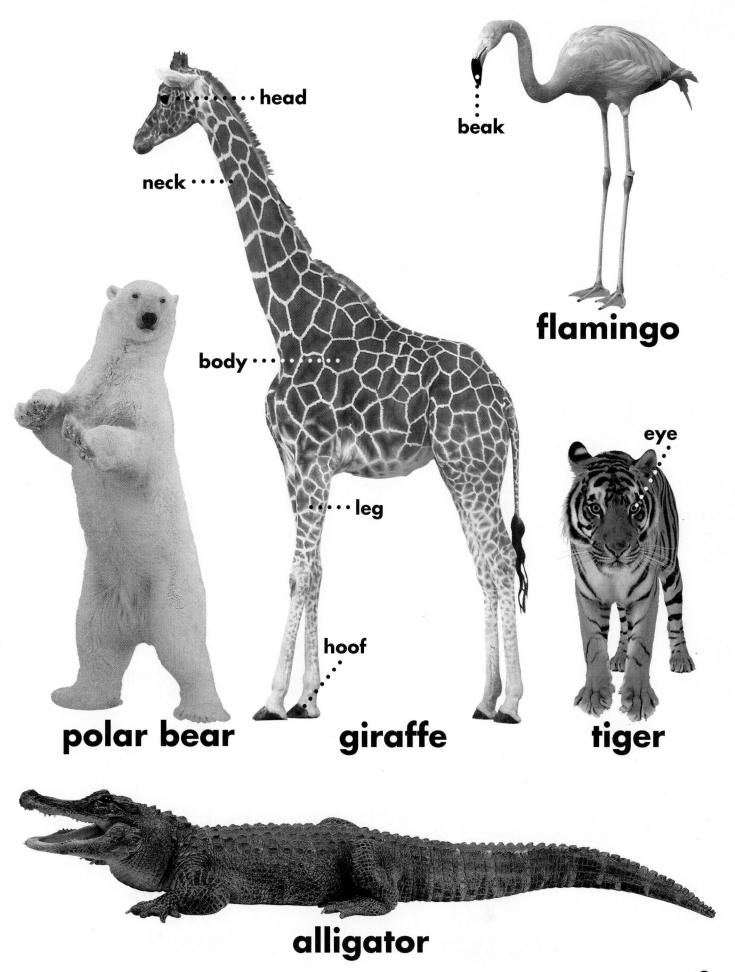

head

beak

neck

flamingo

body

eye

leg

hoof

polar bear **giraffe** **tiger**

alligator

3

Bugs

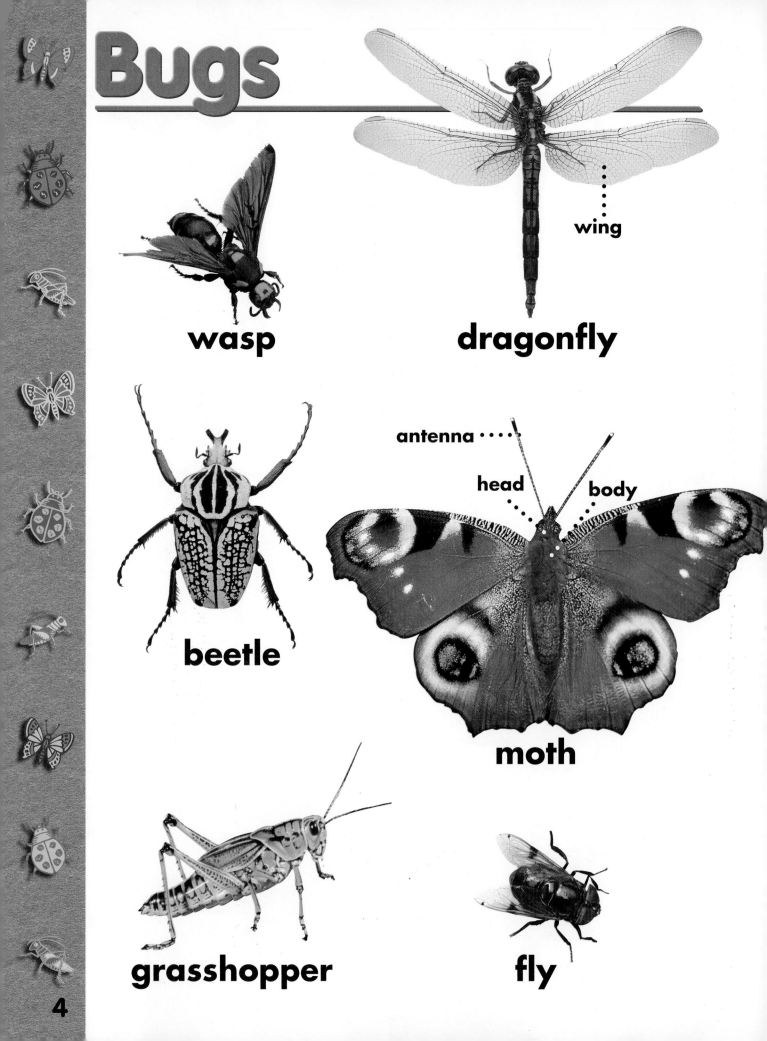

wasp

dragonfly

wing

beetle

antenna

head

body

moth

grasshopper

fly

4

Where do bugs live?

beehive ·······

bee

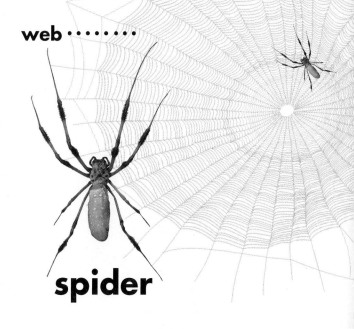

web ·······

spider

shell

snail

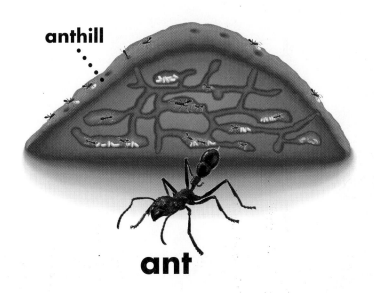

anthill

ant

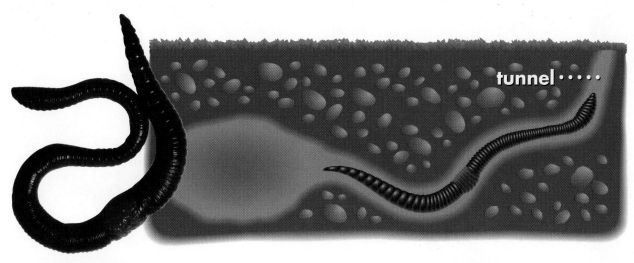

tunnel ·····

worm

5

Celebrations

What are they doing?

candle

lighting candles

hat

dancing

birthday cake

blowing out candles

turkey

sharing a meal

6

wearing special clothes

tuxedo bouquet veil

getting married

ribbon

opening gifts

plume

SANTA ANA WINDS

SANTA ANA, CALIF

marching in a parade

City

school crossing

cone

traffic light

building · street · skyscraper

crosswalk · sidewalk

fire hydrant

stop sign

parking meters

Colors · Shapes

 red

 green

 yellow

 blue

 black

 brown

 purple

 orange

 white

 pink

 tan

 gray

rectangle

circle

.... corner

square

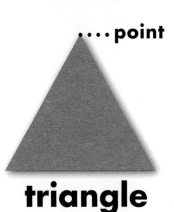

.... point

triangle

9

Day and Night

blanket

teddy bear

waking up

shoes

socks

getting dressed

milk

cereal

orange juice

bananas

eating breakfast

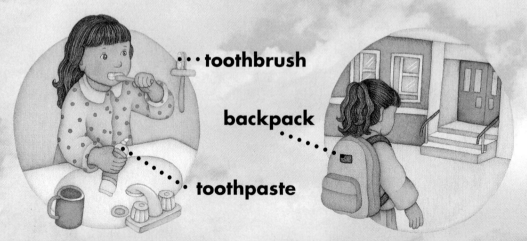

toothbrush

toothpaste

brushing teeth

backpack

going to school

10

drawing pictures

paper

napkin

silverware

plate

setting the table

salad

milk

meat

eating dinner

soap

shampoo

taking a bath

pillow

sleeping

11

Earth

Forest

the planet Earth

trees

bear

squirrel

woodpecker

wolf

moose

skunk

river   fish

12

Ocean

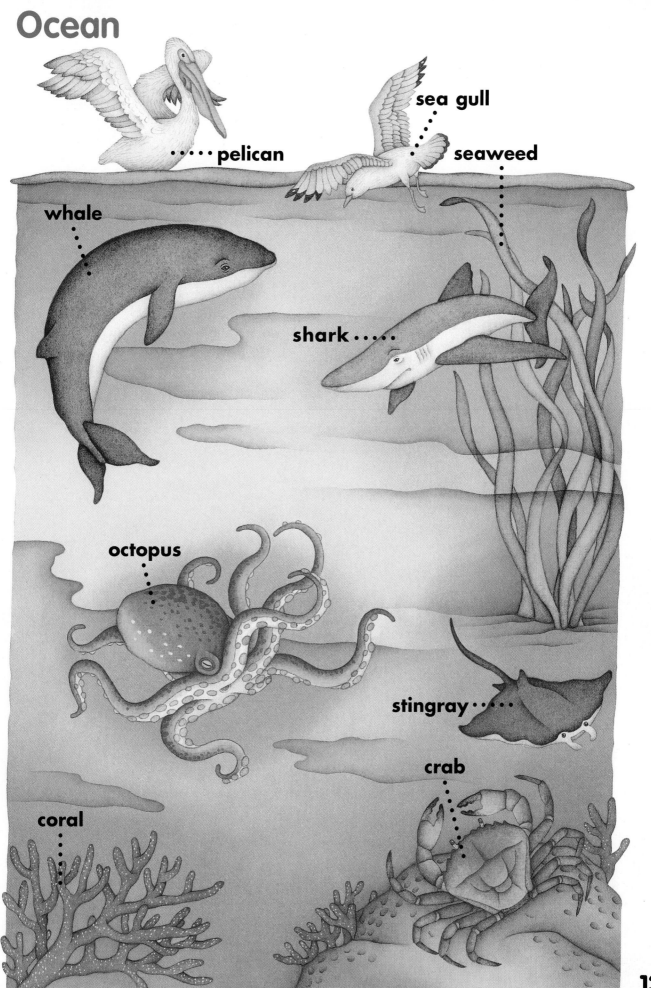

pelican

sea gull

seaweed

whale

shark

octopus

stingray

crab

coral

13

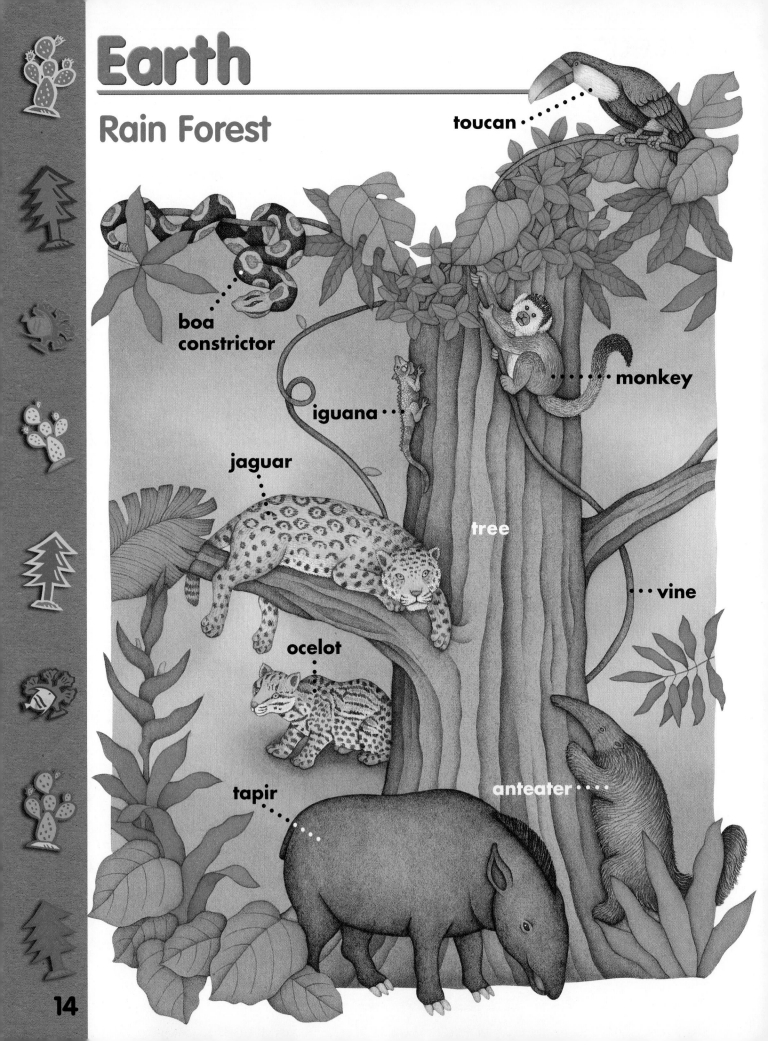

Earth
Rain Forest

toucan

boa constrictor

iguana

monkey

jaguar

tree

vine

ocelot

anteater

tapir

14

Desert

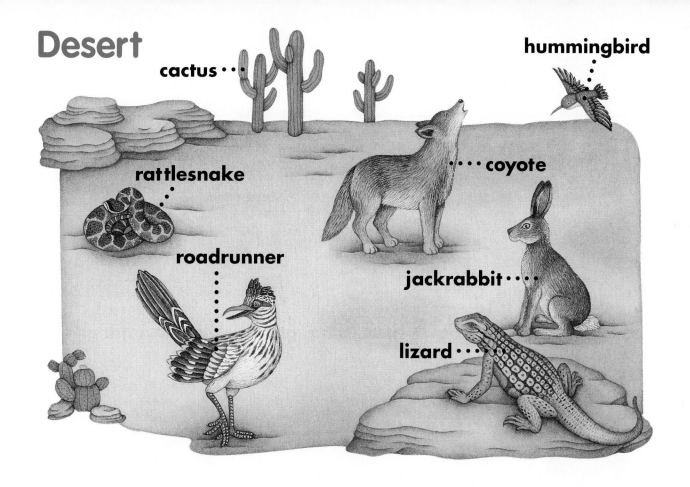

cactus

hummingbird

rattlesnake

coyote

roadrunner

jackrabbit

lizard

Marsh

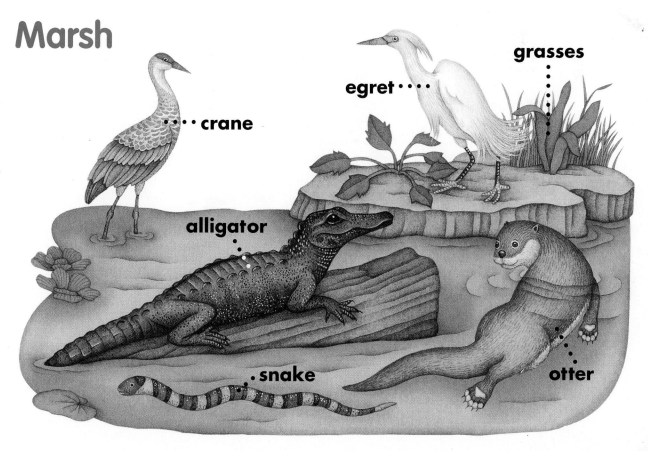

crane

egret

grasses

alligator

snake

otter

Families

The Delgado Family

my grandpa   **my grandma**   **my grandfather**   **my grandmother**

my aunt   **my uncle**   **my mother**   **my father**

my cousin   **my sister**   **my brother**

me

What do families do together?

granddaughter   grandma

look at photos

daughter   mom

read a book

sisters

cook

parents

go on a picnic

dad

have fun

mama

son

hug

Farm

silo

farmhouse

··· **gate**

fence

corral

barn

garden

field

tractor

plow

····· **wheelbarrow**

farmers

Farm Animals

chicks

hen

rooster

sheep

goat

duck

pig

cow

Farm Crops

lettuce

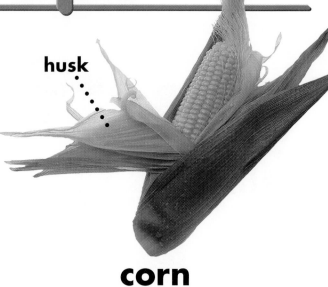

husk

corn

peel

banana

tomato

broccoli

stem

chile

20

cucumber

wheat field

wheat

flesh   seeds

rind

cantaloupe

orange grove

orange

eggplant

pumpkin patch

pumpkin

rice paddy

string beans

rice

21

Food

salad

drumstick

chicken

baked potato

corn-on-the-cob

noodle

soup

bun

meat

hamburger

rice and beans

tortilla

taco

22

Breads

roll

cracker

pita bread

corn bread

sweet bread

biscuit

Desserts

rice pudding

cookies

fresh fruit

pie

cake

custard

23

Friends

What are the friends doing?

digging

shovel

seeds

planting

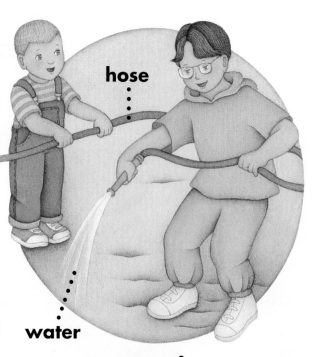

hose

water

watering

weed

pulling weeds

hoe

hoeing

clippers

cutting flowers

roses

tulips

daisies

daffodils

giving flowers to a friend

Growth

Frogs

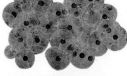

tail

1. eggs   **2. tadpole**   **3. frog**

Butterflies

1. egg   **2. caterpillar**

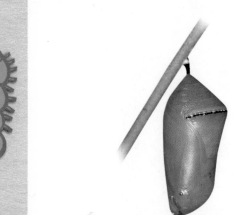

3. chrysalis   **4. butterfly**

Chickens

1. egg **2. chick** **3. chicken**

Pea Plants

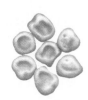

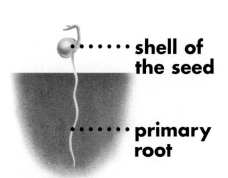

shell of
the seed

primary
root

leaf

1. seeds **2. sprout** **3. seedling**

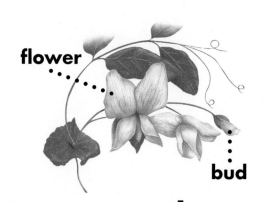

flower

bud

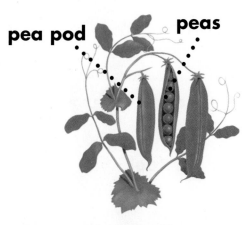

pea pod

peas

4. young plant **5. adult plant**

Healthy Body

Your Body

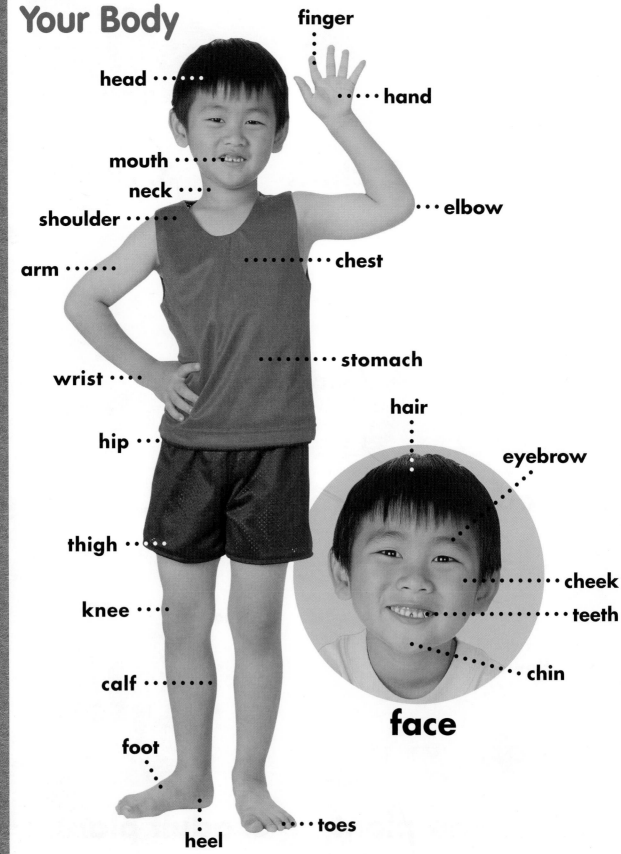

finger

head · · · · ·

mouth · · · · ·

neck · · · ·

shoulder · · · · ·

arm · · · · · ·

wrist · · · ·

hip · · · ·

thigh · · · ·

knee · · · ·

calf · · · · · ·

foot

heel · · · toes

hand

elbow

chest

stomach

hair

eyebrow

cheek

teeth

chin

face

28

How can you stay healthy?

· · · · · apple

eat healthy foods

· · · · helmet

ride a bike

walk

play basketball

swim

get enough sleep

29

mobile home

apartments

wooden house

straw

mud

mud house

yurt

houseboat

adobe homes

log cabin

grass roof

thatched house

cliff

cliff dwelling

stilt

house on stilts

tent

Homes

Inside a Home

window

floor

bedroom

bed

nightstand

desk

chest of
drawers

shower

bathmat

bathroom

toilet

sink

mirror

faucet

bathtub

kitchen

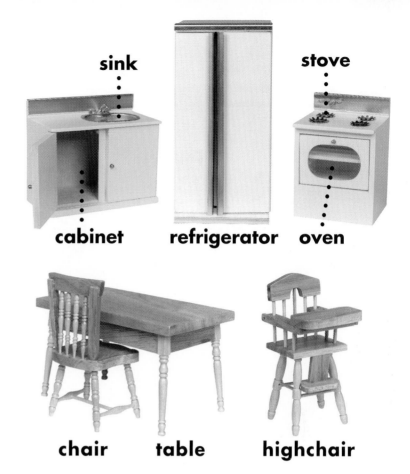

sink

stove

cabinet   refrigerator   oven

chair   table   highchair

wall

coffee table

living room

shelves   television

sofa   easy chair

rug   lamp

33

Neighborhood

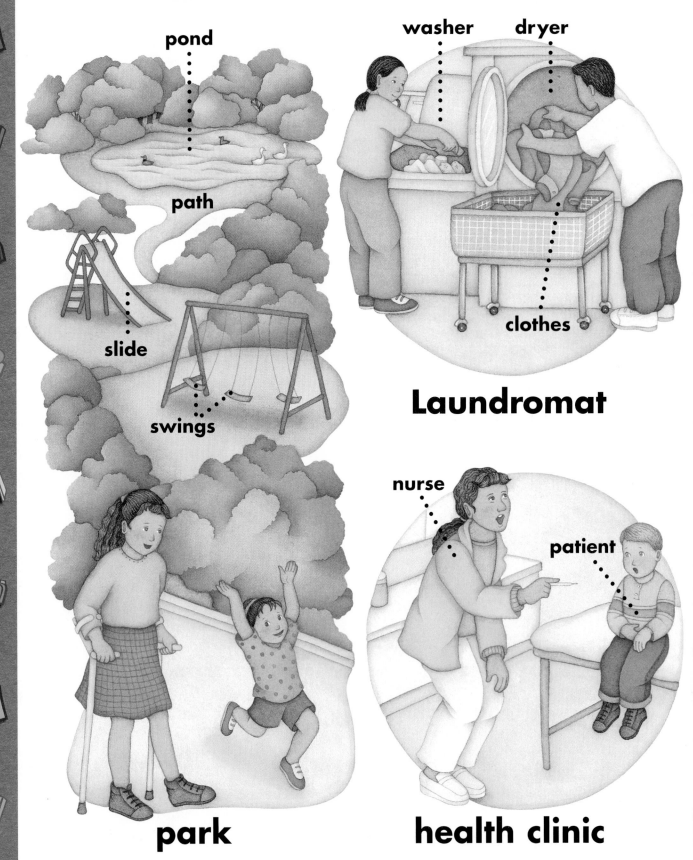

pond

path

slide

swings

washer

dryer

clothes

Laundromat

nurse

patient

park

health clinic

house

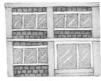
apartments

store

school

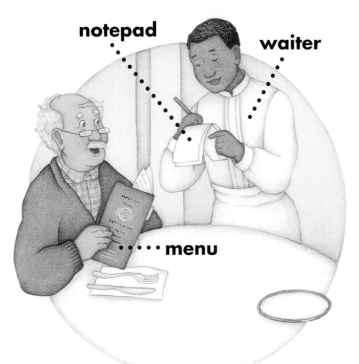

notepad

waiter

menu

restaurant

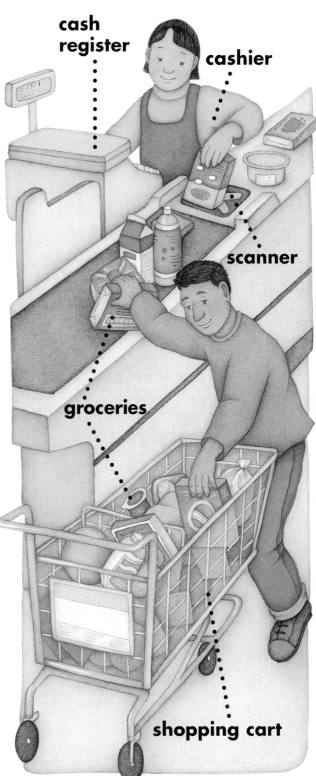

cash register

cashier

scanner

groceries

shopping cart

grocery store

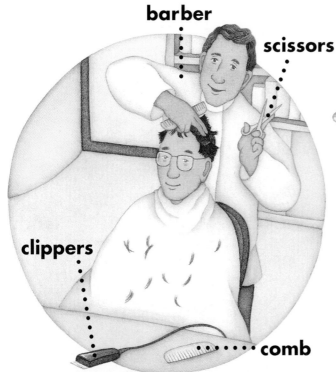

barber

scissors

clippers

comb

barber shop

35

Numbers

1 **one** .... dog biscuit

2 **two**

3 **three**

4 **four**

5 **five**

6 **six**

7 **seven**

8 **eight**

9 **nine**

10 **ten**

first
second
third
fourth
fifth
sixth
seventh
eighth
ninth
tenth

Opposites

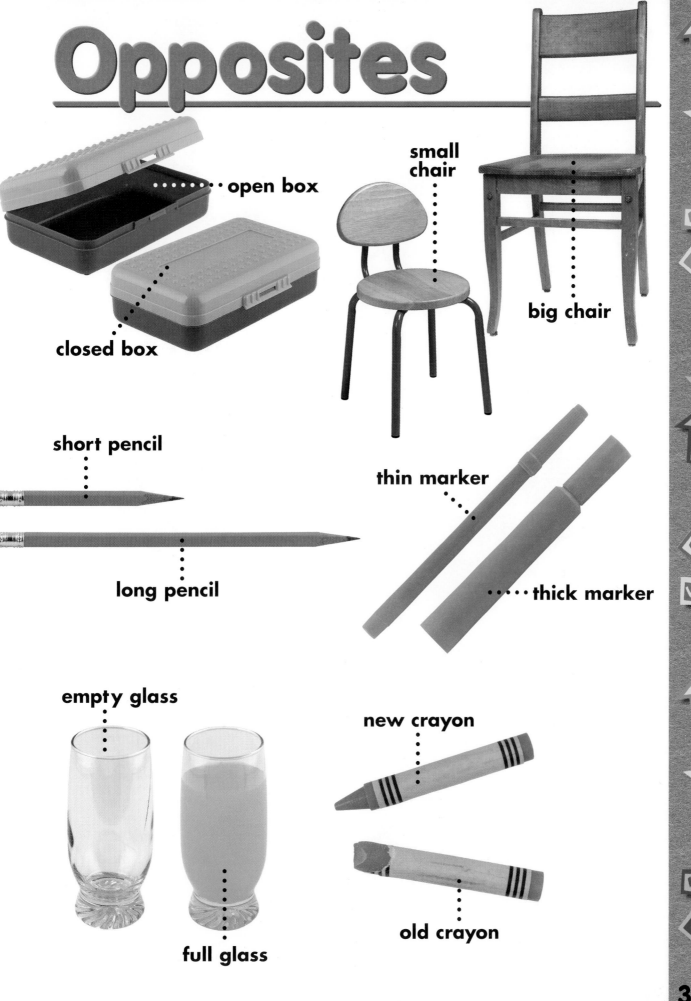

open box

closed box

small chair

big chair

short pencil

long pencil

thin marker

thick marker

empty glass

full glass

new crayon

old crayon

People

boy · · · ·

· · · · · · girl

baby

toddler

children

twins

teenager

man

woman

adults

elder

How do they feel?

angry

happy

scared

yawn

tired

surprised

Pets

whiskers

goldfish

fur

cat

hamster

parrot

feathers

claw

rabbit

shell

tail

turtle

What do dogs need?

food
bowl

dog
leash
exercise

love

brush
collar
brushing

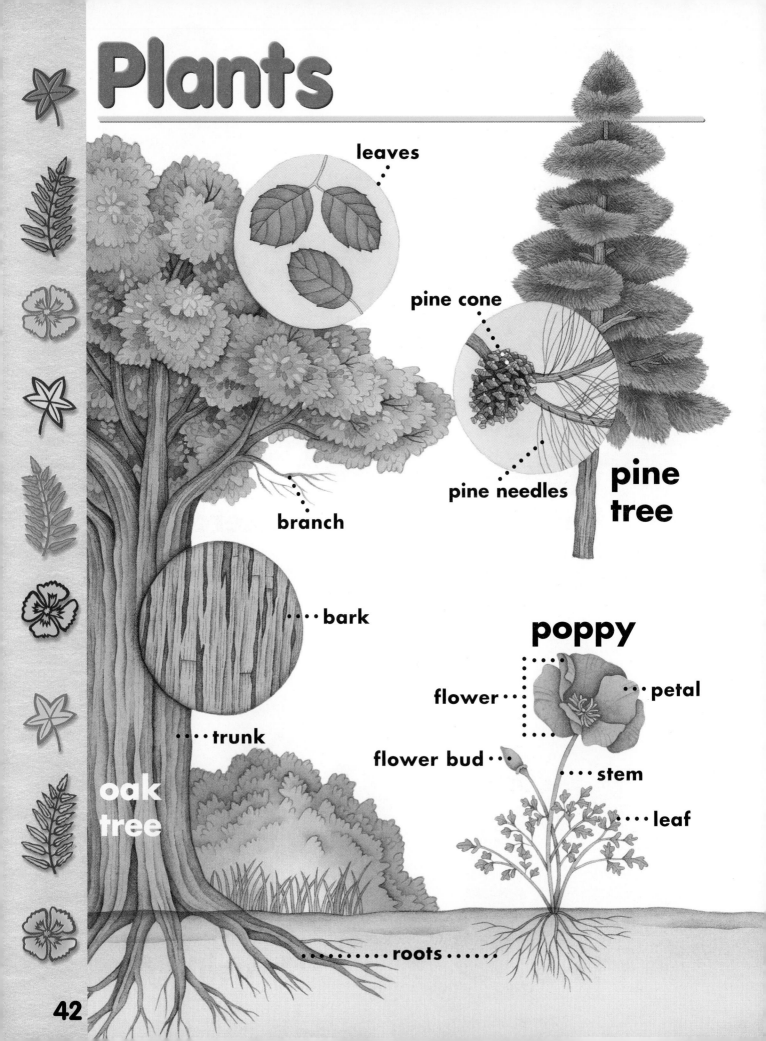

Plants

leaves

pine cone

pine needles

pine tree

branch

bark

poppy

flower · · · · petal

flower bud · · ·

trunk

stem

leaf

oak tree

· · · · · · · roots · · · · · ·

42

Reuse

paper

old milk carton · · ·

bird feeder

glass

used jar · · · · ·

vase

cans

used can · · · · ·

pencils

pencil holder

Seasons

It's Fall. Where's Nam?

at his desk

by the tree

in the kitchen

September   **October**   **November**

It's Winter. Where's Luisa?

over the puddle

behind the snowman

next to the fire

December   **January**   **February**

It's Spring. Where's Tina?

between
the flowers

outside
the bus

under
the kite

March

April

May

It's Summer. Where's Eric?

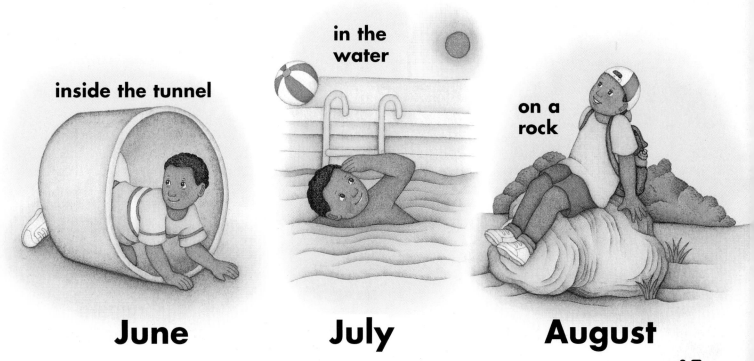

in the
water

inside the tunnel

on a
rock

June

July

August

Senses

Eyes for Seeing

shiny penny

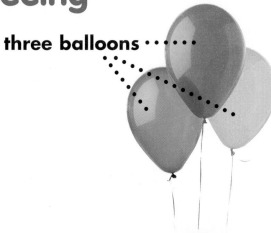

three balloons

striped shirt

round ball

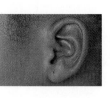

Ears for Hearing

ticking clock

loud whistle

ringing telephone

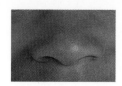
Nose for Smelling

smelly garbage

fresh popcorn

fragrant
flower

Mouth for Tasting

salty pretzel

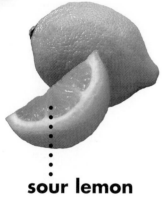

sour lemon

sweet strawberry

Hands for Touching

rough wood

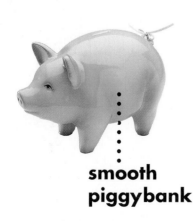

smooth
piggybank

soft rabbit

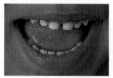

47

Time

Calendar

month ·····
year ·····

January 2001

····· days of the week ·····

Sunday	Monday	Tuesday	Wednesday	Thursday	Friday	Saturday
date ···	1	2	3	4	5	6
7	8	9	10	11	12	13
14	15	16	17	18	19	20
21	22	23	24	25	26	27
28	29	30	31			

Hours of the Day

1 o'clock

2 o'clock

3 o'clock

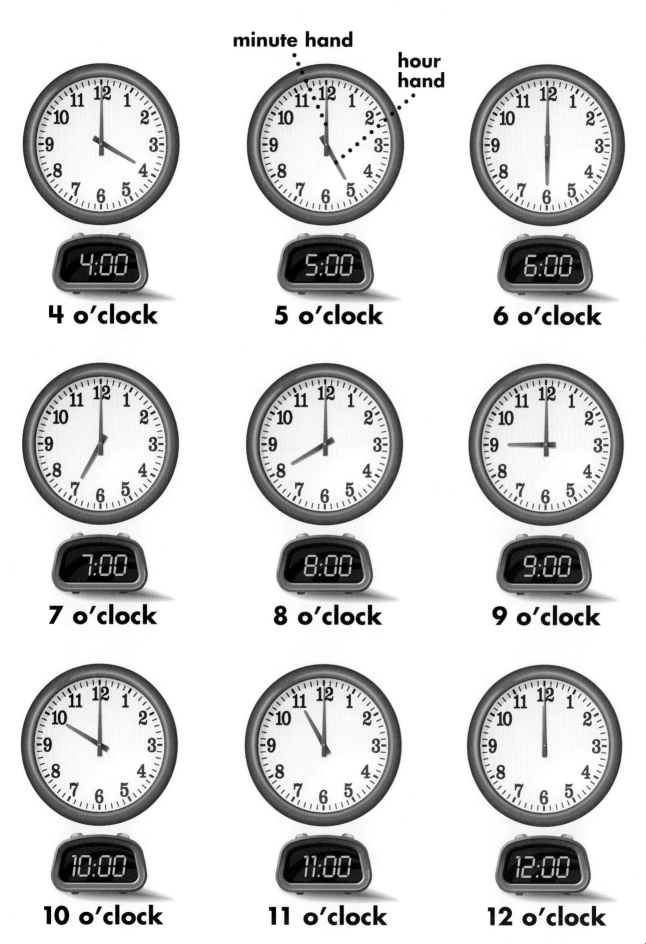

minute hand

hour hand

4:00

4 o'clock

5:00

5 o'clock

6:00

6 o'clock

7:00

7 o'clock

8:00

8 o'clock

9:00

9 o'clock

10:00

10 o'clock

11:00

11 o'clock

12:00

12 o'clock

Transportation

By Air

airplane

helicopter

By Land

train

bus

car

motorcycle

bicycle

jet

rocket

space shuttle

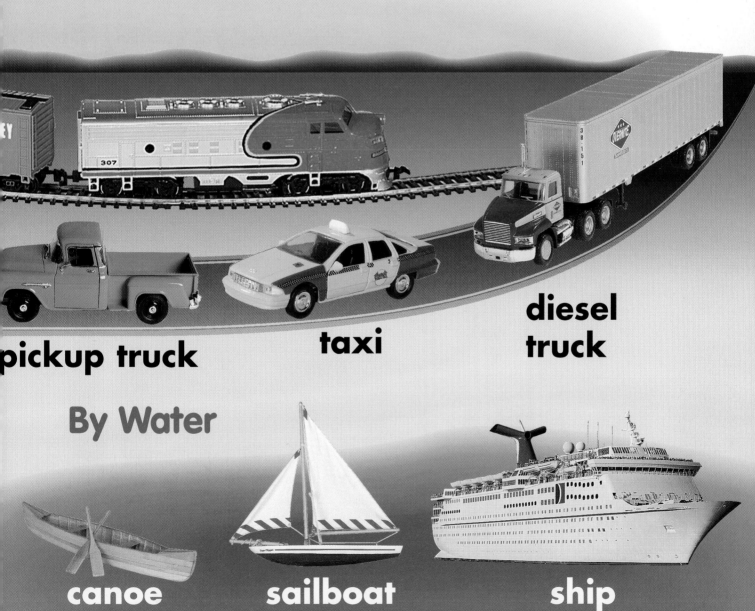

pickup truck

taxi

diesel
truck

By Water

canoe

sailboat

ship

Weather

sun

cloud

What's the weather like?

jacket

pants

stormy

WEEKEND OUTLOOK
HIGHS SATURDAY
0s
10s
20s
30s
70s
THU JAN 5
Temp: 26°F
Wind Chill 30s 7°F
3:36:11 PM

**weather
reporter**

raincoat

boot

rainy

T-shirt

jeans

cloudy

wind

rain

lightning

snow

coat

mitten

cold and snowy

scarf

sweater

windy

blouse

skirt

warm

hat

shorts

sandal

hot and sunny

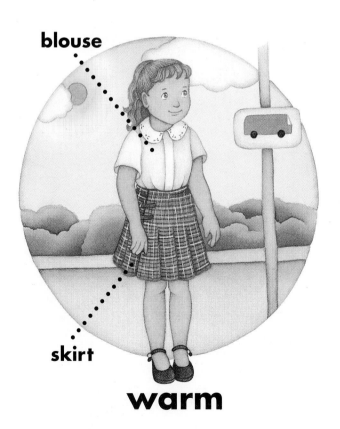

53

Workers

police officer

doctor

bus driver

letter

letter carrier

fire truck
fire hose

firefighters

books

librarian

54

teacher

eraser   chalk   chalkboard

pot

cook

board

carpenter

wrench

plumber

clipboard

office workers

55

Word-Finder Index

Word-Finder Index

Word-Finder Index

Word-Finder Index

62